A Guide for Using

Tuck Everlasting

in the Classroom

Based on the novel written by Natalie Babbitt

This guide written by **Caroline Nakajima**

Teacher Created Materials, Inc.
6421 Industry Way
Westminster, CA 92683
www.teachercreated.com
©1992 Teacher Created Materials
Reprinted, 2004
Made in U.S.A.
ISBN 1-55734-408-6

Edited by
Patricia Miriani

Illustrated by
Sue Fullam

Table of Contents

Introduction

A good book can touch our lives like a good friend. Within its pages are words and characters that can inspire us to achieve our highest ideals. We can turn to it for companionship, recreation, comfort, and guidance. It can also give us a cherished story to hold in our hearts forever.

In Literature Units, great care has been taken to select books that are sure to become good friends!

Teachers who use this literature unit will find the following features to supplement their own valuable ideas.

- Sample Lesson Plans

- Pre-reading Activities

- A Biographical Sketch and Picture of the Author

- A Book Summary

- Vocabulary Lists and Suggested Vocabulary Activities

- Chapters grouped for study, with each section including:
  - *quizzes*
  - *hands–on projects*
  - *cooperative learning activities*
  - *cross–curriculum connections*
  - extensions into the reader's own life

- Post-reading Activities

- Book Report Ideas

- Research Ideas

- A Culminating Activity

- Three Different Options for Unit Tests

- Bibliography

- Answer Key

We are confident this unit will be a valuable addition to your lesson planning, and hope that as you use our ideas, your students will increase their circle of "friends" that they can have in books.

Sample Lesson Plan

Each of the lessons suggested below can take from one to several days to complete.

Lesson 1
- Have students complete the Anticipation Guide on page 8. (See Pre-reading Activity #1, page 7.)
- Read About the Author with your students. (page 5)
- Read the "Prologue" with your students. Establish Active Comprehension questions as a class for reading (See Pre-reading Activity #2, page 7.)
- Begin Reading Response Journals. (page 12)
- Introduce the vocabulary list for Section I. (page 9)
- Assign Word Detective worksheet (page 11) to be used while reading Section I.

Lesson 2
- Read Chapters 1 through 5.
- Go over Word Detective worksheet and discuss meanings of words.
- Vocabulary Activity. (page 10)
- Discuss music boxes and have a Music Box Show. (page 14)
- Work in small groups to develop Feeling—Saying comments. (page 15)
- Do watercolors project. (page 16)
- Lesson on talking about things that might be bothering you. (page 17)
- Administer Section I quiz. (page 13)
- Refer to the list of Active Comprehension questions for reading. Which ones are answered? Add any new questions.
- Introduce vocabulary for Section II. (page 8)
- Assign Word Detective worksheet. (page 11)

Lesson 3
- Read Chapters 6 through 11.
- Go over Word Detective worksheet and discuss meaning of words.
- Vocabulary Activity. (page 10)
- Discuss travel brochures and make one for Treegap. (page 19)
- Discuss myths and beliefs. Do the activity. (page 20)
- Discuss figurative language and do the activity. (page 21)
- Lesson on getting along with people. (page 22)
- Administer Section II quiz. (page 18)
- Refer to the list of Active Comprehension questions for reading. Which ones are answered? Add any new questions.
- Introduce vocabulary for Section III. (page 8)
- Assign Word Detective worksheet. (page 11)

Lesson 4
- Read Chapters 12 through 18.
- Go over Word Detective worksheet and discuss meaning of words.

- Vocabulary Activity. (page 10)
- Learn about terrariums and have students make their own. (page 24)
- Do P. S. Write Back. (page 25)
- Discuss math activity on distance/time/rate.(page 26)
- Lesson on dealing with death. Do activity. (page 27)
- Administer Section III quiz. (page 23)
- Refer to the list of Active Comprehension questions for reading. Which ones are answered? Add any new questions.
- Introduce vocabulary for Section IV. (page 8)
- Assign Word Detective worksheet. (page 11)

Lesson 5
- Read Chapters 19 through 25.
- Go over Word Detective worksheet and discuss meaning of words.
- Vocabulary Activity. (page 10)
- Do Acrostics. (page 29)
- Do "In the News" activity. (page 30)
- Lesson on standing up for what you believe. (page 32)
- Administer Section IV quiz. (page 28)
- Refer to the list of Active Comprehension questions for reading. Which ones are answered? Add any new questions.

Lesson 6
- Read the Epilogue.
- Refer to the list of Active Comprehension questions for reading. Which ones were answered? Are there any questions that were left unanswered?
- Build model cities. (page 34)
- Have a debate. (page 35)
- Make a time line. (page 36)
- Lesson on being the best one can be and goal setting. (page 37)
- Administer Section V quiz. (page 33)
- Have students complete the Anticipation Guide again. Compare results to the first guide.

Lesson 7
- Assign Writing Ideas (page 38)
- Assign book reports. (page 39)
- Assign research projects. (page 40)
- Begin culminating activity. (pages 41-42)

Lesson 8
- Administer Unit Tests 1, 2, and/or 3. (page 43-45)
- Discuss test results and responses.
- Discuss the students' enjoyment of the book

About the Author

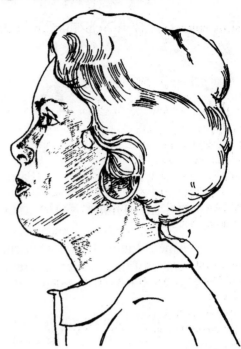

Natalie Babbitt was born in Dayton, Ohio, on July 28, 1932, to Ralph Zane and Genevieve Moore. She attended Laurel School for Girls in Cleveland and went on to Smith College in Northhampton, Massachusetts, receiving her Bachelor of Arts degree in 1954. In that same year she married Samuel F. Babbitt who was the vice-president of Brown University. They have two sons and a daughter.

Babbitt began her career as an illustrator for one of her husband's books. Because her husband soon could not find the time to continue writing, she decided to write and illustrate her own stories. Her success as a writer is evident in the many awards and honors she has received:

- *The Search for Delicious* was the *New York Times* Best Book of 1969 for children ages 9-12;

- *Kneeknock Rise* was an American Library Association (ALA) Notable Book for 1970, a John Newberry Honor Book for 1971, and on the *Horn Book* honors list;

- *Goody Hall* was named a Children's Spring Book Festival Honor Book by *Book World* in 1971, and Children's Book Council Showcase title in 1972, and on the *School Library Journal* list;

- *The Devil's Storybook* was an ALA Notable Book, on the *School Library Journal's* best of the year list, on the *Horn Book* honor list, and a National Book Award nominee;

- *The Eyes of the Amaryllis* was an ALA Notable Book;

- *Tuck Everlasting* was an ALA Notable Book, on the *Horn Book* honor list, received the Christopher Award for juvenile fiction, on the International Reading Association choices list, a U.S. Honor Book, and chosen for the Congress of the International Board on Books for Young People in 1978.

Natalie Babbitt's writing carries messages which are philosophical statements about "human ways, needs and oddities as visible to children as to adults." She has said, "I believe that children are far more perceptive and wise than American books give them credit for being." This belief underlies all of her writing which is original and intelligent and makes it appealing to readers of all ages.

---

[1]'Quotes and information taken from *Twentieth-Century Children's Writers*, D. L. Kirkpatrick, Editor, St. Martin's Press, 1978; and *Contemporary Authors New Revision Series, Volume 19*, Linda Metzger, Editor, Gale Research Company, 1987.

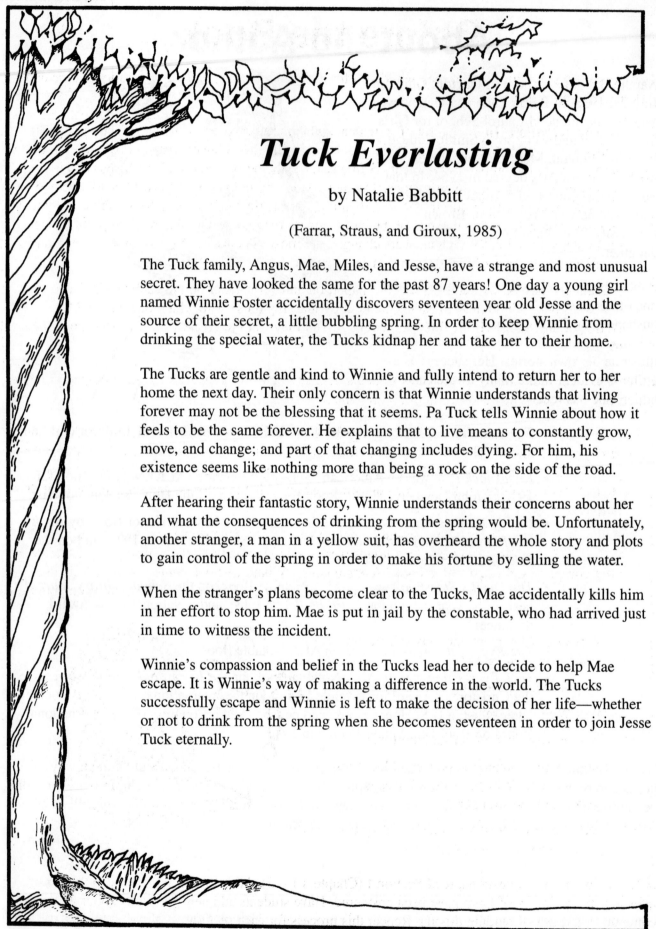

Tuck Everlasting

by Natalie Babbitt

(Farrar, Straus, and Giroux, 1985)

The Tuck family, Angus, Mae, Miles, and Jesse, have a strange and most unusual secret. They have looked the same for the past 87 years! One day a young girl named Winnie Foster accidentally discovers seventeen year old Jesse and the source of their secret, a little bubbling spring. In order to keep Winnie from drinking the special water, the Tucks kidnap her and take her to their home.

The Tucks are gentle and kind to Winnie and fully intend to return her to her home the next day. Their only concern is that Winnie understands that living forever may not be the blessing that it seems. Pa Tuck tells Winnie about how it feels to be the same forever. He explains that to live means to constantly grow, move, and change; and part of that changing includes dying. For him, his existence seems like nothing more than being a rock on the side of the road.

After hearing their fantastic story, Winnie understands their concerns about her and what the consequences of drinking from the spring would be. Unfortunately, another stranger, a man in a yellow suit, has overheard the whole story and plots to gain control of the spring in order to make his fortune by selling the water.

When the stranger's plans become clear to the Tucks, Mae accidentally kills him in her effort to stop him. Mae is put in jail by the constable, who had arrived just in time to witness the incident.

Winnie's compassion and belief in the Tucks lead her to decide to help Mae escape. It is Winnie's way of making a difference in the world. The Tucks successfully escape and Winnie is left to make the decision of her life—whether or not to drink from the spring when she becomes seventeen in order to join Jesse Tuck eternally.

6

Before the Book

Two pre-reading activities which may work well for *Tuck Everlasting* are the Anticipation Guide and Active Comprehension.

1. **The Anticipation Guide** is a set of statements which are designed to challenge and/or support students' current beliefs about the topic which they will read. Students respond by agreeing or disagreeing with the prepared statements before reading the book. Have students discuss their responses and give their justifications. The discussion will help establish prior knowledge and motivate students to get into the book. When the book is finished, go back to the same statements and have students respond again. Graph and compare the results. Did this book have an influence on students' thinking? Which answers changed the most? The least? Discuss the responses and justifications in light of the ideas and insights gained from reading the story.

   Statements may be written on a sheet of paper, on an overhead, or on the chalkboard. Have students respond individually to each statement by marking those with which they agree. One Anticipation Guide is done for you on page 8. You may want to create your own to reflect other ideas.

Extension: After reading the book, have students develop their own questions for an anticipation guide which can be used by the next group to use the unit.

2. **Active Comprehension** is more of an on-going activity to be used not only before reading, but throughout the book. The idea is to have students formulate their own questions about the story prior to their reading. At first, the teacher may need to model some questions, but eventually students will be able to ask their own questions which puts the emphasis on reading for their own purposes.

   Begin by reading the Prologue. Discuss what makes the prologue so well written. Does it hook the reader? How? What writing techniques were used? Do you think the author wrote it before or after completing the rest of the book? Ask students, "What questions come to mind?" List the questions on chart paper. If students are having difficulty coming up with questions, you could use any of the following to get them started:

   - Why does Mae meet her sons at Treegap wood every ten years?

   - Why is Winnie thinking of running away?

   - Will Winnie run away?

   - Whom was the stranger looking for?

   - What is the connection between Mae Tuck and her sons, Winnie Foster of Treegap wood, and the stranger?

   - Will the characters do something they are going to be sorry for later?

After getting a set of questions, read Section I (Chapters 1 – 5). At that point refer back to the list of questions to see if any of them have been answered. Have students add new questions about what has come up as a result of reading this far. Repeat this process for each section.

Anticipation Guide

Put an X in front of those statements with which you agree.

_____ It would be wonderful to live forever.

_____ Everyone who commits a crime must be punished.

_____ People should have control over life and death.

_____ Living means always changing.

_____ Whenever you see an opportunity to make money, you should take it.

In this space, choose a statement that you agree with, and write a paragraph stating the reasons. If you do not agree with any of the statements, write a paragraph stating why you disagree.

_____

_____

_____

_____

_____

_____

_____

_____

_____

_____

_____

_____

_____

_____

_____

_____

Vocabulary Lists

On this page are vocabulary lists which correspond to each sectional grouping of chapters. Choose words that are appropriate to the group's ability. Vocabulary activity ideas can be found on page 10 of this book. Vocabulary knowledge may be evaluated by including the words on the quizzes and tests. This can be done with matching, multiple choice, or fill-in-the-blank type questions.

Section I
Chapters 1- 5

tangent	tolerantly
ambled	exasperated
tranquil	self-deprecation
bovine	remnants
contemplation	gall
infinite	disheartened
veered	consolingly
melancholy	plaintively
ceased	staggering
jaunty	seized
reluctantly	intense
brooch	oppressive
gallows	meager
accessible	dimensions
isolation	stationary
intrusions	

Section II
Chapters 6 -11

troupe	burly
perversely	faltered
elated	receded
reservoirs	indomitable
eddies	perilous
lolled	cavernous
camphor	enveloped
assaults	homely
helter-skelter	kingfisher
disarray	bridle
revolutionary	comprehend
populated	luxurious
source	parson
vanity	vigorous
revived	penetrate
rutted	

Section III
Chapters 12 -18

disarray	silty
lingered	illiterates
constable	roust
cahoots	stern (boat)
threadbare	peril
searing	silhouettes
rigid	willy-nilly
anguish	ordeal
fragrant	accommodations
wheezed	rapidly
flapjacks	

Section IV
Chapters 19 - 25

petulance	unflinchingly
acrid	remorseless
gentility	prostrate
ebbed	furrowed
flailing	accomplice
tarnation	ignorant
mantel	custody
hearth	ghastly
wistful	staunchly
revulsion	

Section V
Epilogue

catholic	verandah	curlicues
chrome	swivel	

9

Vocabulary Activity Ideas

Here are some activities that can be used to help your students learn and retain the vocabulary in *Tuck Everlasting*

❑ Find the sentence in the book with the given vocabulary word. Copy it. Rewrite the sentence by **Substituting a Synonym** which would make sense. The worksheet on page 11 may be used for this activity.

❑ Ask your students to make their own **Crossword Puzzles** or **Wordsearch Puzzles** using the vocabulary words from the story. Have them exchange papers and work the puzzle. When completed, the authors can correct the papers.

❑ Make up sentences for each word, but leave the word out. Trade papers and have the partner **Fill in the Blanks.**

❑ **Fictionary** can be played as a way of introducing new vocabulary. Establish small groups of 4 to 6 students. You will need note paper of uniform size and color. Someone in the group becomes "IT." IT writes down the correct definition of a word from the dictionary on a slip of paper, plus a fictional definition on another slip of paper. Each group member makes up a possible definition and writes it on a slip of paper. Try to make all the definitions sound official. IT collects and shuffles all the definitions. Then IT reads the definitions and the other group members must guess the correct definition. IT receives one point for each group member he successfully "stumps," and awards group members one point for guessing the correct definition. Play then moves to the next person on the left to be IT.

❑ Use the words and definitions to play **Bingo.** Fold an 8 ½" x 11" paper into 16 squares. Have students randomly write the words chosen for this activity in each space. The caller reads a definition and the players mark the correct word. Markers can be pieces of cut index cards, beans, or raisins. The first person to cover a row, column or diagonal calls out Bingo and is the winner.

❑ Play **Hangman** using the definition as a clue. This might be a good activity to be played in partners.

❑ Challenge your students to a **Vocabulary Bee!** This is similar to a spelling bee, but in addition to spelling each word correctly, the game participants must correctly define the words as well.

❑ Challenge your students to use a specific vocabulary word from the story at least 10 **Times In One Day.** They must keep a record of when, how, and why the word was used!

❑ As a group activity, have students work together to create an **Illustrated Dictionary** of the vocabulary words.

❑ Play **20 Clues** with the entire class. In this game, one student selects a vocabulary word and gives clues about this word, one by one, until someone in the class can guess the word.

❑ Play **Vocabulary Charades.** In this game, vocabulary words are acted out.

Word Detective

For each vocabulary word, hunt through the section in the book for the word and copy the sentence in which you find it on the first line. Then, on the second line, rewrite the sentence using a synonym or phrase that would make sense and keep the same meaning.

WORD   **SENTENCES**

WORD	SENTENCES
	1. _____ _____ 2. _____ _____
	1. _____ _____ 2. _____ _____
	1. _____ _____ 2. _____ _____
	1. _____ _____ 2. _____ _____
	1. _____ _____ 2. _____ _____

Reading Response Journals

As your students read through *Tuck Everlasting,* have them keep a Reading Response Journal. Reading journals are a wonderful way for students to make the personal connections that reading literature is all about.

To create the journal, have students assemble lined and unlined paper in a cover. The cover can be a simple 12" x 18" construction paper folded in half, or it can be made more sophisticated by using a regular report cover found in stationery stores. They may want to draw a design for the cover or simply title it and add their name.

Tell them that the purpose of the journal is for them to record their reactions, feelings, ideas, observations, and questions that come up as they read the story. They might want to copy a favorite sentence or key passage.

You may want to provide questions or relevant topics for students to respond to in order to stimulate writing. For example:

Section I: Have you ever felt like running away like Winnie? Why or why not?

Section II: Tell about a time when you were told a fantastic story that was supposed to be true, and you were not sure whether or not to believe it.

Section III: What do you think about what Winnie said, "It'd be nice if nothing ever had to die"?

Section IV: Think about a time when you had to make a very hard decision. What did you do?

Section V: Where do you think you will be 10 years from now? What do you think you will be doing?

Sometimes students may want to respond to their reading by drawing a picture instead of writing. Have them use the blank pages to do so.

Tell them that they may share their responses with their classmates if they wish. Sharing is a great way to stimulate discussions and broaden points of view.

Emphasize that they will not be graded on grammar, punctuation, or spelling, but that effort is what is important.

Encourage students to expand their journal ideas into stories, essays, poems, and art displays.

Provide time for students to write in their journals daily.

Try to read journals regularly. Since emphasis is on content, not style or grammar, no corrections should be made. Respond by making nonjudgmental and encouraging comments or asking questions such as, "That's an interesting idea!" or "Do you think you might want that to happen to you?" If grades are given, they should be based on effort and number of entries.

Quiz Time!

1. On the back of this paper, write a description of each of the characters introduced in this section. Provide as much detail as possible about their physical characteristics, relationships, and personalities.

2. What does the "touch-me-not appearance" of the cottage mean?

   _____

   _____

3. Describe the woods next to the cottage.

   _____

   _____

4. What amazing fact about the Tucks is revealed?

   _____

   _____

5. Describe Mae's one special object. _____

   _____

6. Why is Winnie thinking about running away? _____

   _____

   _____

7. What two comments did Winnie's grandmother make about the music coming from the wood?

   _____

   _____

8. What do you think the man in the yellow suit wants? _____

   _____

   _____

9. What happened in the wood when Winnie went there in the morning?

   _____

   _____

10. What do you think Mae Tuck meant when she said, "Well, boys, here it is. The worst is happening at last"? _____

    _____

    _____

Music Boxes

Mae Tuck had a little music box which she took with her wherever she went. It was very special to her. Swiss music boxes of the late 1800's, like Mae's, can be considered one of the earliest types of mechanical instruments for the home. In 1877, Thomas Edison invented the speaking phonograph which recorded and reproduced voices at home. It used a cylinder similar to the one in the music box, but instead of pins attached, grooves were made as one cranked the cylinder and talked. Because the music boxes were expensive and limited to only a few tunes, by the early 1900's, people were using disc phonographs and talking machines which led to record players, tape recorders, and all the electronic instruments we use today.

Nevertheless, music boxes have remained popular as collector items. There is something enchanting about music boxes which makes them appealing to people of all ages. They come in all shapes, sizes, and sounds. Learn how they are made. What makes the music? How does it work? Consider a player piano—is it a giant music box?

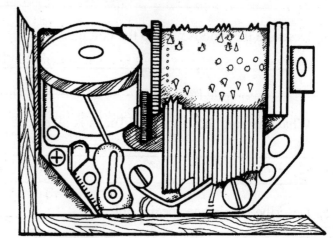

Challenge students to make their own music "boxes". Encourage creativity. These can be as simple as a music box made from rubber bands or as elaborate as a decorated box housing an instrument or radio. Have a Music Box Show. Each student brings in a music box. Music boxes can be the ones that students made or real ones. Display them. Group the student-made music boxes into categories such as most creative, most beautiful, best music, etc. Group the "real" ones into categories such as ceramic, wood, children's toys, holidays, size, type of music, or any other appropriate category. Have students give a demonstration of their music boxes. Let each talk about where it came from and if it has a special meaning.

Feeling—Saying

" 'All right! I'm coming!' she cried, exasperated, and then added quickly, 'I mean, I'll be right there, Mama.' "

Like Winnie, how many times have you done the same thing, especially with your parents, where you feel one way but say another? It often happens when we know we must do something, but really don't want to.

Working in small groups of 4 or 5 students, look through magazines for pictures in which you can think up comments to add—one for what the person might be feeling and one for what he/she actually says. Write your comments on a blank piece of paper, cut them out in the shape of cartoon bubbles, and glue them onto your picture. Working together, you should be able to come up with some very witty ideas!

These may be compiled into a class book entitled "That's What You Think." Students may also choose to act out scenarios, prerecording their thoughts or having someone narrate.

Art: Water Colors

Reread the description of the woods at the beginning of Chapter 5. Close your eyes and envision what it looks like. Paint your idea of the woods using watercolors.

Using watercolors is a technique that is free flowing and enjoyable. Its beauty lies in its transparency of colors and the appearance of spontaneity. Before painting the impressions of the Treegap wood, you may want to review and practice some watercolor techniques which the students can use in their picture.

There are two paper methods of using watercolor paints: wet, and dry. The wet paper method requires putting on a clear water wash before adding the color. This method makes the edges of the color very soft. Conversely, the dry paper method is putting the colors directly on dry paper. These two methods can be used alone or together in the same paintings.

On the brush, using a lot of water will make a color transparent while a little dampness will create bold and heavy colors. Leaving white paper showing through as part of a picture is also an effective technique in watercolor painting.

In creating colors for the picture, colors can be blended right on the picture as well as beforehand on the palette. Sometimes the overlapping of transparent colors will automatically create a new color. For this reason it is best to work from light colors to dark.

Have students try out different strokes, colors, and methods on practice paper in order to become comfortable with the medium. Then, as they get started with their painting, remind them that if they use pencil underdrawings, keep them very light and simple because they will show through. Change the dipping water frequently to keep the colors pure. And finally, the best watercolor paintings look as if they were painted very quickly, even though a great deal of thought and planning went into them.

Talking About It

Winnie was tired of all the directions she got from her mother and grandmother. She felt like she had no chance to be herself and do what she wanted to do. The only friend she had to talk to was the toad, but at least she was able to let her feelings out.

In our own lives things happen that make us upset, anxious, and angry. We need someone to help us out, to give us support by listening, comforting, advising, and caring. It might be a close friend, a sister or brother, a parent, a relative, a teacher, or a counselor. Like Winnie, it might even be a pet that can at least listen and comfort.

Write a letter to someone that you know would listen to you. Tell about what is bothering you and how it makes you feel, or tell them how they have helped by listening to you in the past.

Note to teacher: Allow students to keep these letters private if they desire. If you feel you must see them, announce that beforehand.

Quiz Time!

1. What was unusual about Winnie's kidnapping?

_____

_____

2. What would you have done in Winnie's place?

_____

_____

3. What did Winnie discover about the music she had heard the night before?

_____

_____

4. What was the fantastic secret the Tucks told Winnie?

_____

_____

5. On the back of this page, list at least five of the nine events that the Tucks revealed as support for their incredible story.

_____

_____

6. Why didn't the Tucks want Winnie to drink from the spring that morning?

_____

_____

7. Why do you think the man with the yellow suit was smiling?

_____

_____

8. How do Jesse's and Miles's views about the spring differ?

_____

_____

9. How was the home lifestyle of the Tucks different from that of the Fosters?

_____

_____

10. Why can't the Tucks stay in any one place for very long?

_____

_____

Travel Brochure

Have students bring in travel brochures that they might have at home. Examine them together and decide on some common characteristics found in all of them such as: pictures, positive features of the area, things to do, places to stay, special activities, maps, advertisements, and endorsements.

From reading the descriptions of Treegap and its surrounding areas, make a travel brochure that would entice tourists to visit the area. Remember to include those things discussed that make a good travel brochure. Use your imagination to expand on the information you have from the story to make people want to take a vacation in Treegap.

Use this outline to organize the information you wish to include in the brochure.

Favorite Beliefs

Winnie's grandmother told her that the elves had returned to the forest. Elves are one of those myths that we want to believe in, but really do not have concrete evidence for their existence.

In small groups have students research the origins and any other information they can locate about the topics presented below. Using the form provided, fill in the information for each topic. Make a cover for them, and create a group booklet. Possible topics for research include:

- Elves
- Loch Ness Monster
- Big Foot

- UFO's
- Ghosts
- Leprechauns

As extensions, research myths or beliefs that are unique to a certain culture, such as Greek mythology. In small groups, write a short play that includes the information from the research, as well as the fictional beliefs. Perform the plays for the class.

Belief _____

Origin or History: _____

_____

Description: _____

_____

Personal Feeling about Belief: _____

_____

Picture

Language Arts: Figurative Language

Tuck Everlasting is made interesting both by its exciting plot and by its use of figurative language. The story is enriched with similies, metaphors, and personification.

A simile compares things to one another by using the word as or like. It helps to better describe how something looks, feels, smells, tastes or sounds by comparing the object to something else with which we are familiar.
Example "...this weary old earth...would have trembled on its axis like a beetle on a pin."

A **metaphor** also compares two different things, but it does not use a word of comparison such as *like* or *as*.
Example: "At this, the toad stirred and blinked. It gave a heave of muscles and plopped its heavy mudball of a body a few inches farther away from her."

Personification is a form of figurative language in which an animal or object is given human characteristics.
Example: "The graceful arms of the pines stretched out protectively in every direction

Listed below are examples of figurative language found in *Tuck Everlasting*. On the space provided by each example, write the name of the type of figurative language.

1. _____   "...a stack of wooden bowls, their sides smoothed to velvet."

2. _____   "...her backbone felt like a pipe full of cold running water..."

3. _____   " 'I'm about dry as dust.' "

4. _____   "So the road went humbly by and made its way..."

5. _____   "But at the same time he had a kind of grace, like a well oiled marionette."

6. _____   "The sun was only just opening its own eye..."

7 _____   "It (the music) was like a ribbon tying her to familiar things."

8. _____   "The last stains of sunset had melted away..."

9. _____   "...enclosed by a capable iron fence some four feet high which clearly said,'Move on—we don't want you here.'"

10. _____   "...the wrinkled surface of a tiny lake..."

11. _____   "The sun was dropping fast now, a soft red sliding egg yolk,..."

12. _____   "...they gathered around her like children at their mother's knee."

Challenge: Find and identify other examples of figurative language from the book.

Getting Along

A unique way to have students participate in sharing ideas is a round table activity. Round table is a small group activity in which there is one piece of paper and one pen for the group. One student starts by writing a contribution on the paper and then passes the paper and pen to the person on his/her left. The paper and pen literally go around the table. Use the suggestions below to guide students.

When Winnie stayed with the Tucks, she saw a lifestyle quite the opposite of her own fastidious one. How did she act with them that showed she cared about their feelings, was open-minded, and accepting of their differences? Make a class list.

In our lives we meet so many people, and everybody is different in some way. As a round table activity, make lists of ways people are different. For example, people are different because of religious beliefs, race, language, dress. How many other ways can you think of? Share the lists with the rest of the class. Then discuss in the groups which reasons are valid basis for rejecting people and which are not, and why. Have one person from each group summarize what was discussed.

After participating in this activity and listening to all the discussions, what advice can you give to someone about meeting new people?

Additional round table topics:

• Advantages to living forever

• Disadvantages to living forever

• Possible uses for the spring water

• Common disagreements between adults and children

Quiz Time!

1. How have Winnie's feelings changed? _____

   _____

2. Describe Angus Tuck. _____

   _____

3. In one sentence tell what Angus Tuck was trying to explain to Winnie at the pond.

   _____

   _____

4. Why did Angus Tuck say that they are "like rocks beside the road"?

   _____

   _____

5. What did Angus Tuck say might happen if everyone found out about the special spring?

   _____

   _____

6. Why do you think the Tucks are so excited and pleased about having Winnie with them?

   _____

   _____

7. What did Jesse ask Winnie to do? _____

   _____

8. Why hadn't Miles taken his wife and children to drink the special water?

   _____

   _____

9. What would happen if nothing ever died?

   _____

   _____

10. What bargain did the man with the yellow suit make with the Fosters?

    _____

    _____

Terrarium

In Chapter 12 Tuck and Winnie go out on the pond to talk about the cycle of life. He says, "Everything's a wheel, turning and turning, never stopping. The frogs is part of it, and the bugs, and the fish, and the wood thrush, too. And people." Tuck is talking about the interrelationships between living things and their environment. The natural balance of all things on earth keeps everything moving and alive. It is an ecosystem.

Make a miniature ecosystem by creating a terrarium. Within the terrarium, all conditions such as humidity, temperature, and soil nutrients are controlled and self-sustaining so that the glass or plastic container becomes the ecosystem for the plants inside it.

Choose plants that have the same kinds of requirements to flourish together inside your terrarium.

Materials needed:

A glass container such as a fish bowl, an old aquarium, a brandy snifter, or a large jar

A cover for the container which can be made of plastic wrap or glass

Coarse gravel

Small plastic screen or charcoal chips

Soil made up of humus, leaf mold, and loam—packaged potting soil works well

Plants; Water mister

Steps in putting together your terrarium:

1. Spread a layer of coarse gravel at the bottom of the container to keep water from settling in the soil.

2. Place a plastic screen or charcoal chips on top of the gravel to separate the soil from the gravel. Charcoal chips will help to keep the soil clean.

3. Decide where you want the plants and carefully place them in the soil with a little clump of their own soil. Plants need to have enough space to grow, so avoid overcrowding.

4. Add moisture by spraying water on the plant leaves with a mister (any spray bottle will do.) The soil should be moist, but not soggy.

5. Put on the cover and watch the terrarium for a few days to adjust the moisture. If it seems too dry, add some mist. If it is too damp and water drops form on the container, then wipe off the glass and leave the cover off for while to dry it out.

6. Place your terrarium where it will get the appropriate amount of light, but won't get too hot.

Once it is established, your terrarium should be able to thrive on its own, and you can enjoy your miniature ecosystem!

P.S. Write Back

In chapter 14, Jesse asks Winnie to drink from the spring when she turns seventeen so they can be together forever. In groups of two to four, write a letter from Jesse to Winnie listing all the reasons why she should drink from the spring, or write a letter from Winnie to Jesse with her decision and the reasons for the choice.

As a whole class, take turns reading the letters aloud, beginning with a letter from Jesse and then reading a response from Winnie. How many groups said yes to Jesse's proposal? How many said no? Discuss which letters gave the most convincing reasons, which were the most original, and which pair of letters fit together the best.

Extension: Divide the class into two groups. Select the members of one group to each write a letter from a character in *Tuck Everlasting* to an advice columnist, and the members of the other group to each write a letter of advice. Since the "advice columnists" won't know what the problem is that they are responding to, they will need to use their creativity to write an answer that will cover almost anything.

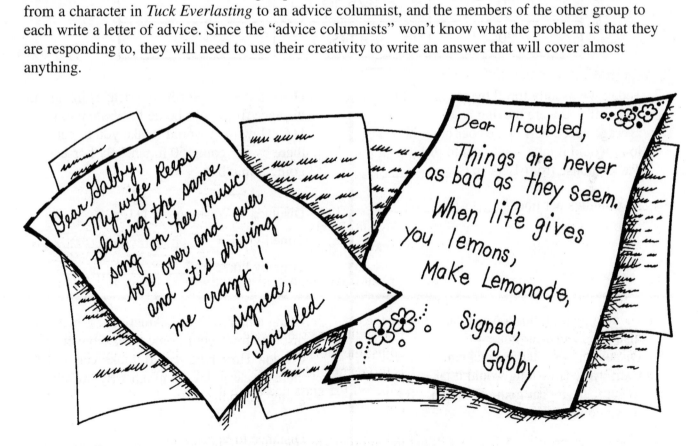

Randomly select one letter from the problem pile, and one from the solution pile, and read them aloud. Discuss which letters were the most amusing and which fit together the best.

Were the students able to guess which characters the letters were from, based on the problems they wrote about?

Math: Distance—Time—Rate

Most of *Tuck Everlasting* is set in the 1880's, a time when people usually depended on horses for transportation. The epilogue takes place in 1950, and although the Tucks continue to use their horse drawn buggy, cars are predominant. Solve the following problems (round to the nearest hundredth). Then compare the speeds of both methods of transportation.

1. It was 20 miles from Treegap to the Tuck's house. The man in the yellow suit and the constable had a 3 or 4 hour ride ahead of them on horseback. Fill in the chart below to tell the speed of the horse for each time listed. (Remember that the rate is calculated by dividing the distance by the time.)

Distance	Time	Rate (m.p.h.)
20	3 hrs.	
20	3.25 hrs.	
20	3.50 hrs.	
20	3.75 hrs.	
20	4 hrs.	

2. Today we usually travel by car to go 20 miles. If you were moving at an average speed of 45 miles per hour, how long would it take you to get to the Tucks' house from Treegap? _____

   At 60 miles per hour? _____

3a. Using a map of North America, estimate the distance from your home to Washington, D.C. How long would it take you to get there by car going 50 m.p.h.? By horse going 5 m.p.h.?

   Distance to Washington, D.C.= _____

   Time by car = _____

   Time by horse = _____

3b. Using a map of North America, estimate the distance from your home to Disneyland, located in Anaheim, California. How long would it take you to get there by car going 50 m.p.h.? By horse going 5 m.p.h.?

   Distance to Disneyland = _____

   Time by car = _____

   Time by horse = _____

3c. Using a map of North America, estimate the distance from your home to Vancouver, Canada. How long would it take you to get there by car going 50 m.p.h.? By horse going 5 m.p.h.?

   Distance to Vancouver= _____

   Time by car = _____

   Time by horse = _____

Poetic Thoughts

Pa Tuck told Winnie, "Dying's part of the wheel right there next to being born." Even though we know it is a natural part of life, it still can be hard to deal with when it touches us personally. The grief we feel is a sign of love and is a very natural feeling. To get through the grief it helps to cry and talk about our feelings and about the person or pet that died. Slowly we come to accept the loss and go on with our lives. Understanding why death is a necessary part of life can help in the healing process, and it also helps us to see the value of life. Perhaps that was what Tuck was trying to convey to Winnie.

Poetry is one avenue that people use to express and make sense of their feelings. We can read the words of other writers, but writing poetry can sometimes be very difficult for people to do completely on their own. However, by *dialoguing* with a poem that's already written, the task can be much easier and fun. Do this activity as a total class. Read the first two lines of the poem. (Usually this activity is done one line at a time, but for this particular poem two lines work better.) Students are to write down exactly what you say. Then students are to write a phrase or sentence that comes to mind in response to the two lines read. Repeat this procedure two lines at a time until the poem is completed.

Choose three students to read their lines as a group poem. Teacher reads the original two lines and students A, B and C read their responses one after the other. Continue in the same way to the end. Then try it with a different group of students. You will be surprised by the rhythm and beauty of the results.

You shall ask

What good are dead leaves

And I will tell you

They nourish the sore earth.

You shall ask

What reason is there for winter

And I will tell you

To bring about new leaves.

You shall ask

Why are the leaves so green

And I will tell you

Because they are rich with life.

You shall ask

Why must summer end

And I will tell you

So that the leaves can die.

by Nancy Wood*

Quiz Time!

1. On the back of this paper, write a summary of the events that occurred in this part of the story.

2. How did the man in the yellow suit know about the Tucks? _____
   _____

3. What clue made it possible for the man to recognize the Tucks?_____
   _____

4. What do you think about the plans of the man in the yellow suit?
   _____
   _____

5. Why did Mae hit the man in the yellow suit?
   _____
   _____

6. Why had Angus Tuck looked at the body of the man on the ground almost enviously?
   _____
   _____

7. Why was it so important that Mae not go to the gallows?
   _____
   _____

8. How did Winnie feel about all that had happened?
   _____
   _____

9. How had Winnie changed since we first met her at the beginning of the book?
   _____
   _____

10. Do you agree with the constable that Winnie is a criminal because she had been an accomplice in
    freeing Mae from jail? Should she be punished? Give reasons for your opinions. _____
    _____
    _____

Acrostics

In an acrostic, the letters of a word or name are written vertically to provide the structure for the poem.

Make an acrostic for each person or place from the story. Think about what each is like. Then write a word that fits that person or place for each letter of the name. Use a thesaurus and/or a dictionary to help you out.

J oyful _____

E nthusiastic _____

S weet on Winnie _____

S eventeen _____

E ager _____

T hin _____

U nsettled _____

C urly hair _____

K ind _____

W _____

I _____

N _____

N _____

I _____

E _____

F _____

O _____

S _____

T _____

E _____

R _____

M _____

I _____

L _____

E _____

S _____

T _____

U _____

C _____

K _____

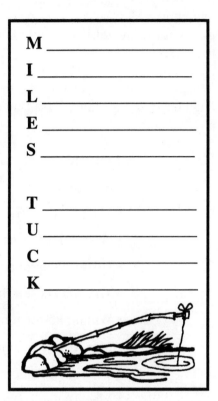

T _____

R _____

E _____

E _____

G _____

A _____

P _____

M _____

A _____

E _____

T _____

U _____

C _____

K _____

A _____

N _____

G _____

U _____

S _____

T _____

U _____

C _____

K _____

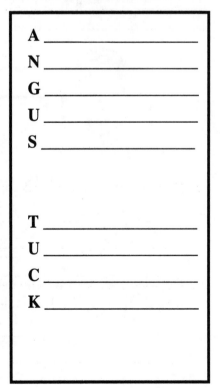

In the News

Divide the class into groups of 7 or 8 students. Each group represents a different TV news broadcast and must choose an event from *Tuck Everlasting* to present on the 5 o'clock news.

Within the group, students can decide on roles to play, such as anchor person, reporter in the field, or people to be interviewed. Prepare scripts, questions, and answers to make the news broadcast as authentic and informative as possible. If a video camera is available, record the newscasts. Students may wish to include introduction music and commercials for products that would have been available in the 1880's.

While one group is performing, the rest of the class must watch for accuracy, completeness, objectivity, and clarity in reporting. Based on that broadcast, would they tune in again tomorrow or change to another channel?

Here are some suggested events to present:

> • Stranger dressed in a yellow suit arrives in Treegap.
>
> • Mysterious activity in the Foster wood.
>
> • Winnie Foster disappears.
>
> • Horse stolen outside of Treegap.
>
> • The Fosters sell their wood.
>
> • Winnie Foster found unharmed.
>
> • Mae Tuck put in jail for murder.
>
> • Unusual summer storm hits Treegap.
>
> • Mae Tuck escapes.

Choose one of the above or think of another event that you would like to present.

Science: Frogs and Toads

What kind of animal is a toad? How is it similar to and different from a frog? Is it true, as Winnie's grandmother said, that toads drink water through their skin? Research these animals to learn about their physical characteristics, eating habits, reproductive cycle, life span; where they fit into the food chain; and the different species of frogs and toads that exist.

Here are some key words to look for:

amphibians	tadpoles	metamorphosis
vocal sacs	species	embryo
algae	predators	prey
hibernation		

Make a chart showing the changes a frog and toad go through from birth to adulthood.

Use the Venn diagram below to list the similarities and differences between frogs and toads.

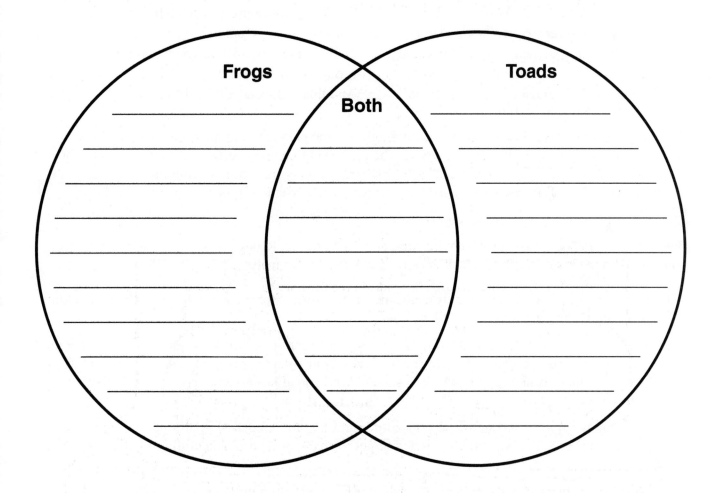

Draw a picture of one species of a frog or toad. Be sure to show as much detail about its shape, colors, and other unique attributes as possible. Label it with its name and some specific information about the species.

Hard Decisions

Winnie had decided that she would help get Mae out of jail, even though she knew her parents wouldn't allow it if they knew. Yet, she "had her own strong sense of rightness," and she believed that this was something she had to do. So, as much as she didn't want to disobey her parents, she decided she would go ahead with her plan, and then make them understand later.

It is easy to do something when there are many people with you, supporting you, agreeing with you. However, when you must do something alone because in your heart you believe it is right, regardless of what others may think, that is truly difficult—but that is also the most rewarding.

Read Robert Frost's poem, "The Road Not Taken"

Two roads diverged in a yellow wood,
And sorry I could not travel both
And be one traveler, long I stood
And looked down one as far as I could
To where it bent in the undergrowth;
Then took the other, as just as fair,
And having perhaps the better claim,
Because it was grassy and wanted wear;
Though as for that the passing there
Had worn them really about the same,

And both that morning equally lay
In leaves no step had trodden black.
Oh, I kept the first for another day!
Yet knowing how way leads on to way,
I doubted if I should ever come back.
I shall be telling this with a sigh
Somewhere ages and ages hence:
Two roads diverged in a wood, and I—
I took the one less traveled by,
And that has made all the difference.

By taking the less traveled road, that is, the midnight escape plan, do you think that Winnie felt it had "made all the difference"? Think about a time when you had to make a difficult decision. It may not have been as dramatic as what Winnie did, but it would certainly have been as important to you. Describe the choice. Tell why it was a difficult decision, what you did, how it turned out, and how you felt about it.

Below are several situations for which there are no easy answers. Read each situation and decide what you would do. Be ready to give reasons for the choices you have made.

1. You see an elderly woman shoplift medication from a drug store. You think she probably couldn't afford to pay for it. Do you report her?

2. Your best friend will fail English if he/she misses one more homework assignment. You know the assignment is done because you saw it completed. Your friend has forgotten the assignment at home, and there is nobody to bring it to school. Your friend has asked to copy your homework. What would you do?

3. Your dog is very old and sick. The vet said it might live for another year or longer but it would probably be in pain. You could have the dog put to sleep, or let it die naturally. What would you do?

4. Your mother has worked very hard after work every night for a month making a Halloween costume for you. You don't like it and suspect you will be teased if you wear it. What would you do?

Quiz Time!

1. Explain what Winnie did to "make a difference in the world."

   _____

   _____

   _____

2.   "Stone walls do not a prison make,
             Nor iron bars a cage."

   What do you think these lines mean in reference to the Tucks?

   _____

   _____

   _____

3. At the end of the story, we see that the toad is still around. By saving the toad from the dog and pouring the special water on it, Winnie was doing something she thought was good. Compare that to what the man with the yellow suit wanted to do.

   _____

   _____

   _____

4. Why do you think that Winnie did not drink from the special spring herself?

   _____

   _____

   _____

5. Explain why Tuck said, "Good girl."

   _____

   _____

   _____

6. What do you think Winnie did the rest of her life?

   _____

   _____

   _____

Your Future City

Treegap certainly has changed from the small town at the beginning of the book to the growing city at the end. What causes cities to change? Population, technology, money, and needs of the people are a few reasons. Can you add to the list?

If you could plan your own city, what are the things you would want to include? Here are a few ideas to consider:

public sectors	communication
private sectors	energy sources
entertainment	water
recreation	food
transportation	waste disposal
shopping	government

Use your imagination. The city does not necessarily have to be on land as we know it today.

Consider the ocean, space, moon, or even other planets. Make a model of your city using cardboard, clay, wood, sticks, boxes, plastic articles, paints, toys, and whatever else you can find to create your ideal city. Be prepared to give an oral explanation of its location, power sources, and environment.

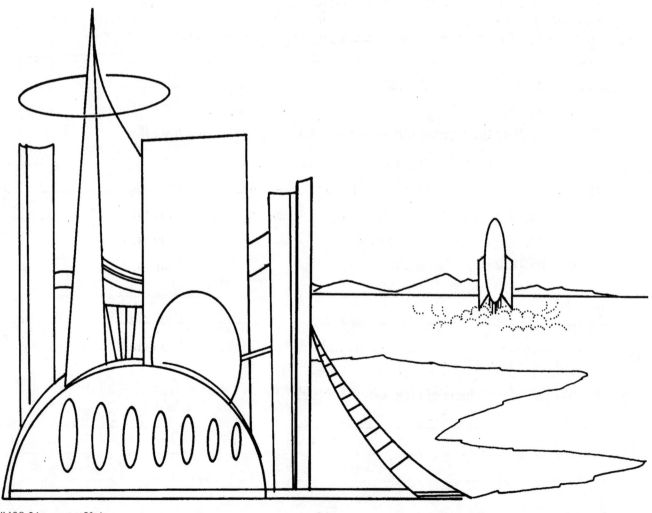

Debating

Tuck Everlasting brings up some issues that are very relevant to our lives today. Because these issues have two sides which can be argued, they lend themselves perfectly to the art of debate. What issues come to your mind after reading this story? Make a list on the board. Here are a few that might be considered:

1. Should there be a death penalty?

2. Should everyone who breaks a law be punished?

3. Should there be socialized medicine?

4. If death is a natural part of life, should we try to prolong life?

5. Does everyone have a right to know everything, or should some things be kept "top secret"?

6. How much interference, if any, should people do to change the environment?

Break into teams of 2 or 3 to take a pro or con position on a topic. Research your topic and be familiar with both positive and negative points. Prepare a short speech to present your position. Be prepared to defend yourself against rebuttals by anticipating what your opponents may say. Have a conclusion prepared which might be adjusted after hearing the actual comments of the opposing side.

The actual debate presentation can be limited to any number of minutes and structured in different ways, but here is a sample framework for teams of 2 members (pro comments should start):

First Pro Opening Statement	5 minutes
First Con Opening Statement	5 minutes
Second Pro Opening Statement	5 minutes
Second Con Opening Statement	5 minutes
(Team members consult about what they heard)	1 minute
Pro Team Rebuttal Comments	3 minutes
Con Team Rebuttal Comments	3 minutes
First Pro Concluding Statement	1 minute
First Con Concluding Statement	1 minute
Second Pro Concluding Statement	1 minute
Second Con Concluding Statement	1 minute

Did anyone in the class change his/her opinion as a result of what was said during the debate?

Social Studies: Time Line

At the time we meet the Tucks the year is 1880. They said they had drunk the spring water 87 years before which would have been in the year 1793. Since Jesse and Miles were 17 and 22 years old, Mae and Pa were probably in their 40s at that time, which means they must have been born sometime around 1750.

In all the years that the Tucks have been alive, they have seen many events and inventions. In small groups, use encyclopedias and other reference books to help write the letter of each event in the box next to the year it occurred on the time line.

A. Martin Luther King Jr. delivers "I Have a Dream" speech

B. Beethoven is born

C. Persian Gulf War

D. Walt Disney is born

E. Telephone is invented

F. First regular T.V. broadcast in the U.S.

G. Ben Franklin performs famous kite experiment

H. Elvis Presley dies

I. Statue of Liberty presented to the United States from France

J. The Beatles debut in the U.S.

K. Declaration of Independence is signed.

L. Orville and Wilbur Wright Kitty Hawk flight

M. Civil War begins

N. Korean War begins

O. Lewis and Clark expedition

P. Women allowed to vote in U.S.

Q. Henry Ford introduces gasoline powered car

R. United States Constitution signed

S. United States involvement in World War II

T. World War I begins

U. The *Challenger* disaster

V. First men to walk on the moon.

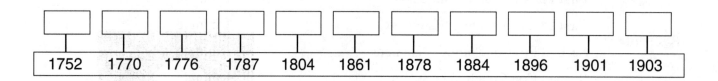

| 1752 | 1770 | 1776 | 1787 | 1804 | 1861 | 1878 | 1884 | 1896 | 1901 | 1903 |

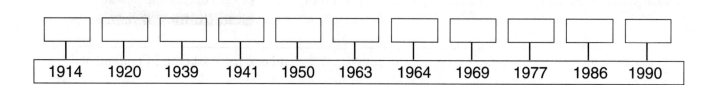

| 1914 | 1920 | 1939 | 1941 | 1950 | 1963 | 1964 | 1969 | 1977 | 1986 | 1990 |

Making a Difference

Miles said to Winnie, "People got to do something useful if they're going to take up space in the world." This is what life is all about, isn't it? "Doing something useful" does not always have to mean being the greatest of leaders in the world, just as long as it is being the best that you can be. Read the following poem:

A Little Fellow Follows Me*

A careful man I want to be,
   A little fellow follows me;
I do not dare to go astray,
   For fear he'll go the self-same way.
I cannot once escape his eyes,
   Whate'er he sees me do, he tries;
Like me he says he's going to be,
   The little chap who follows me.

He thinks that I am good and fine,
   Believes in every word of mine;
The base in me he must not see,
   The little chap who follows me.
I must remember as I go,
   Through summer's sun and winter's snow,
I am building for the years to be
   That little chap who follows me.

Who might the "little fellow" be? Could it be a younger sister or brother, students in the lower grades, or children around the neighborhood? As you grow, there will always be someone following you who will be looking up to you whether you realize it or not. So, what we do in our lives is important.

Think about your goals, both short and long term. What things do you want to accomplish?

It might be as simple as remembering to keep your room clean or learning or improving a skill. Whatever you want to do, write here. Keep the list to look at from time to time to see how you are doing in meeting these goals and revise them as you grow and change.

Short Term Goals

This week:_____

This school year:_____

Long Term Goals

Next five years: _____

Someday in the future: _____

Remember:

   "If you can't be a highway, then just be a trail,
   If you can't be a sun be a star;
   It isn't by size that you win or fail,
   Be the best of whatever you are.

---

*Taken from John Wooden's favorite poems in his *Player's Notebook* for Basketball Fundamentals Camp. Reprinted with permission.

Writing Ideas

These suggestions may be used for Reading Response Journal topics, daily writing assignments, or as discussion questions.

- What if another group of people also discovered the spring? Write a story telling about their experiences.

- Retell the story from the point of view of one of the characters. Some suggestions include the toad, the man in the yellow suit, the constable, or Winnie's grandmother.

- Do you think the Tuck family would still have taken the drink from the spring if they had known it would cause them to live forever? Explain your answer.

- If Winnie had used the water to join Jesse eternally, do you think they would have wanted their children to drink the spring water? Explain your answer.

- Describe how the world might be different if the man in the yellow suit had survived and gone ahead with his plan.

- Are there any ways the Tuck family could have been destroyed? Write about possible attempts and the probable results.

- Invent a new kind of magic spring. What happens to the people who drink from it? Some ideas may include flying, becoming invisible or reading people's minds. Write a story describing the adventures of a person who drinks from the new spring.

- Write about an encounter Miles might have with one of his grandchildren.

- Write an interview with a member of the Tuck family describing his/her feelings about living forever.

- Think about an occupation that the Tucks might be good at. Write a story describing a typical day on the job.

- How do you think the spring got its magic power? Write a story describing the origin of the spring.

- Rewrite an episode of a favorite T.V. show, having one or all of the Tucks as guest stars.

- How do you think the story would have been different if the man in the yellow suit had not found Winnie and the Tucks?

- What if the Tucks discover a spring that makes them mortal? Would they drink from it? How would their lives change?

Book Report Ideas

There are numerous ways to do a book report. After you have finished reading *Tuck Everlasting* choose one method of reporting that interests you. It may be a way that your teacher suggests, an idea of your own, or one of the ways below.

- **Board Game**

  Make a board game based on the events of *Tuck Everlasting*. Lay out the spaces on a piece of construction paper or tagboard. You might want to add comments here and there on the spaces for interest, such as: Lose one turn, Go back 3 spaces, or Move forward 1 space. Then decorate around the spaces with scenes from the book. Make a set of at least 25 game cards, each with a question about the story. Make an answer key on a separate sheet of paper in order to check responses during the game. You will need dice and a colored marker for each player. To play, the players must answer a question correctly in order to throw the dice and move. The first person to reach the Finish is the winner!

- **Filmstrip**

  Make a filmstrip or "roller movie" of the story of *Tuck Everlasting*. Draw pictures of all the significant events of the story and "roll it" as you narrate. If blank filmstrips are available, use colored markers for drawing and present your work on the screen. If not, use a roll of paper such as computer paper rolled onto a dowel on each end. Cut a "screen" into an appropriate size box. Insert the dowels on the top and bottom from the back so that they can be turned to create a "roller movie" which can be narrated.

- **Literary Critic**

  Be a literary critic and write a book review of *Tuck Everlasting*. Include a brief summary of the story and your opinion on the strengths and weaknesses of the plot, characters, and writing style. Tell whether or not you recommend this book to other readers.

- **Book Jacket**

  You are the publisher of the book *Tuck Everlasting*. Design a book jacket that will attract attention and encourage people to pick up the book and want to read it.

- **TV Commercial**

  With other students, as many as necessary, create and perform a TV commercial to sell the book. Make your commercial entertaining and to the point.

- **Letter to the Author**

  Write a letter to Natalie Babbitt and tell her what you thought about *Tuck Everlasting*. Include specific points about what you liked most or least. Ask any questions that came to mind as you read the book. You may want to ask questions about being a writer and how she got the idea for this story. After your teacher has read it, and you have made your writing the best it can be, send it to her in care of the publishing company.

- **Performing**

  Act out a scene from *Tuck Everlasting*. You may need to ask some fellow students to help you out by being other characters. Explain why you chose the scene and why it is important to the story.

- **Model**

  Construct a 3-dimensional model of your favorite scene from *Tuck Everlasting*. Give an oral explanation of the scene and why you chose it.

Research Ideas

Describe three things you read about in *Tuck Everlasting* that you would like to learn more about.

1. _____

2. _____

3. _____

Although *Tuck Everlasting* is a fictional story, there are many ideas and facts that bring up questions and suggest topics for further study. Researching and developing a better understanding of such topics enhance one's appreciation of the book and its author. Work in groups to research one or more of the areas you named above, or the areas that are mentioned below. Share your findings with the rest of the class in any appropriate form of oral presentation.

- Cycle of life
- Causes of aging
- Preserving youthfulness in the cosmetic industry
- Medical technologies in prolonging life
- Capital punishment
- Human behavior
- Amphibians
- Pond life
- Plant and animal life
  - Native to your home area
  - Plant varieties and required environments
  - Animal habitats
- Underground springs
- Weather
- Ecology
- Future cities
- Historical development of cities
- Development of music machines
- Development of automobiles
- Choose an event from your class time line to expand upon
- Fishing
- Horseback riding

40

Story Diagram

There is often a basic pattern to the action of a story line. One such pattern can be shown as a W:

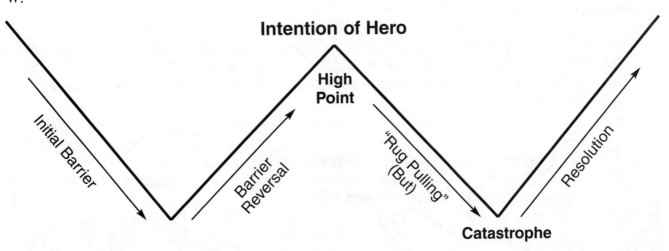

Think about the story of Cinderella. It could be diagrammed as follows:

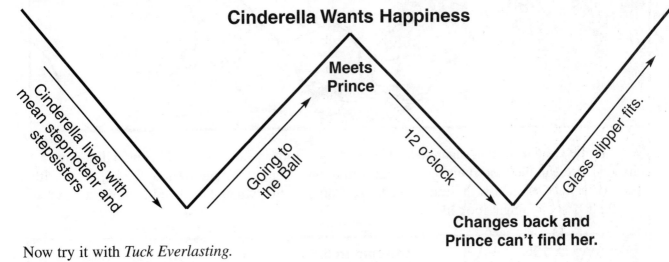

Now try it with *Tuck Everlasting.*

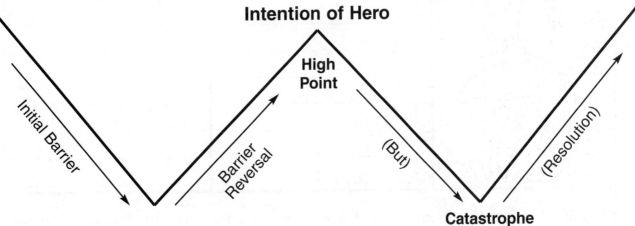

On the back of this page, answer the following:

Do you think Winnie made the right decision? Why or why not? What is the author's point of view? Support your answers with specifics from the book.

What If?

As a culminating activity, have your students do some speculating and creative thinking. Have them do some "What if" reflecting about Winnie, Treegap, and the Tucks. This is an opportunity to let their imaginations soar.

1. What if Winnie had decided to drink some of the special spring water? How would the story have changed? When do you think she drank it? Did she wait until she was 17?
   How would her decision affect her family, the wood, and Treegap? Brainstorm your ideas and then write a new ending to this story.

2. What if you were to visit Treegap today? What do you think you would find? How will it have changed? Reread the descriptions of Treegap, first, on the night Winnie went to the jailhouse with Jesse (Chapter 24), then at the end of the book. Compare the two and then add a third list of what you think Treegap might look like today.

Treegap in 1880	Treegap in 1950	Treegap Today

3. What if you met the Tucks tomorrow and they told you their fantastic story? Would you believe them? How would you decide if it was true? What would you do?

   Write a story describing the circumstances of your meeting. Tell what they look like and what they say to you. Explain your reactions and what becomes of them and you.

Unit Test

Matching: Match these quotes with the characters who said them.

Winnie	Mae	Tuck	Jesse	Man in Yellow Suit

1. _____ "It's no use having that dream. Nothing's going to change."

2. _____ " I want to grow again, and change. And if that means I got to move on at the end of it, then I want that, too...."

3. _____ ". . . Why, heck, Winnie, life's to enjoy yourself, isn't it? What else is it good for? That's what I say. . ."

4. _____ "I can't think why you're so upset. Did you really believe you could keep that water for yourselves? . . ."

5. _____ "I'm not exactly sure what I'd do, you know, but something interesting— something that's all mine."

True or False: Write true or false next to each statement below.

1. _____ Jesse wanted Winnie to wait until she was older to drink from the spring.

2. _____ Miles's wife knew the stranger's grandmother.

3. _____ The Tucks were foolish old people.

4. _____ The stranger had a good idea.

5. _____ Winnie was able to make a difference in the world.

Short Answer: Provide a short answer for each of these questions.

1. When Winnie was first taken away by the Tucks, what helped to calm her down?

    _____

2. How did the Tucks know that it was the water from the spring that caused them to stop changing?

    _____

3. How did the man in the yellow suit find Winnie?_____

4. How did the constable know that Mae should be arrested? _____

5. What helped the escape plan work? _____

Essay: Answer the essay questions on the back of this paper.

1. Do you think Winnie made the right decision? Why or why not? What is the author's point of view? Support your answers with specifics from the book.

2. What do you think Winnie gained from her experience?

Contrasts

Tuck Everlasting deals with many contrasting elements. Write specifics from the story which support the contrast listed.

Example:

life *The Tucks were alive-they could not die* _____

death *Winnie eventually died.* _____

1. right _____

   wrong _____

2. young _____

   old _____

3. moving _____

   still _____

4. changing _____

   unchanging _____

5. neat _____

   messy _____

6. happy _____

   sad _____

7. mortality _____

   immortality _____

8. love _____

   hate _____

9. selfish _____

   giving _____

10. choice _____

    no choice _____

Response

Explain the meaning of the following quotations from *Tuck Everlasting*.

Chapter 1: "Nothing ever seems interesting when it belongs to you—only when it doesn't."

Chapter 2: "'I was having that dream again, the good one where we're all in heaven and never heard of Treegap.'"

Chapter 3: "'I'm not exactly sure what I'd do, you know, but something interesting something that's all mine. Something that would make some kind of difference in the world.'"

Chapter 4: "'Did you hear that, Winifred? That's it! That's the elf music I told you about. Why, it's been ages since I heard it last. And this is the first time you've ever heard it, isn't it?'"

Chapter 5: "It was one thing to talk about being by yourself, doing important things, but quite another when the opportunity arose. The characters in the stories she read always seemed to go off without a thought or care, but in real life—well, the world was a dangerous place."

Chapter 7: "It was the strangest story Winnie had ever heard."

Chapter 8: "They made her feel old. And the way they spoke to her, the way they looked at her, made her feel special. Important. It was a warm, spreading feeling, entirely new."

Chapter 9: "'Well, then,' Tuck repeated, 'seeing you know, I'll go on and say this is the finest thing that's happened in—oh—at least eighty years.'"

Chapter 12: "'Life, moving, growing, changing, never the same two minutes together.'"

Chapter 12: "'Being part of the whole thing, that's the blessing.'"

Chapter 15: "'I've got what you want, and you've got what I want.'"

Chapter 19: "'But I'm not going to sell it to just anybody,' he protested. 'Only to certain people, people who deserve it. And it will be very, very expensive. But who wouldn't give a fortune to live forever?'"

Chapter 20: "Mae Tuck must never go to the gallows."

Chapter 23: "When she was seventeen—would she?"

Epilogue:
　　　"In Loving Memory
　　Winifred Foster Jackson
　　　　Dear Wife
　　　　Dear Mother"

Epilogue: "'Durn fool thing must think it's going to live forever,' he said to Mae."

Bibliography

Nonfiction

Anderson, Lydia. *Death.* (Franklin Watts, 1980)

Baldwin, Dorothy. *Health and Friends.* (Rourke Enterprises, Inc., 1987)

Brennan, Matthew J. *The Environment and You.* (Grosset & Dunlap, 1972)

Gatland, Kenneth & David Jefferis. *The World of the Future Future Cities.* (Usborne Publishing, 1979)

Hoke, John. *Terrariums.* (Franklin Watts,Inc.,1972)

Hoover, Cynthia. *The History of Music Machines.* (Drake Publishers, Inc., 1975)

Royston, Robert. *Cities 2000.* (Facts On File Publications, 1985)

Sayer, James Edward. *Argumentation and Debate Principles and Applications.* (Alfred Publishing Co., Inc., 1980)

Yerian, Cameron and Margaret. *Fun Time Indoor Gardening.* (Childrens Press, 1975)

Zaidenberg, Arthur. *How to Paint with Water Colors A Book for Beginners.* (Vanguard Press, 1968)

Fiction

Babbit, Natalie. (Farrar, Strauss, & Giroux, Inc.)

  Search for Delicious (1969)

  Kneeknock Rise (1984)

  Goody Hall (1971)

  The Devil's Storybook (1974)

  The Devil's Other Storybook (1987)

  The Eyes of the Amaryllis (1977)

Barrie, J.M. *Peter Pan.* (Holt, 1987)

Coblentz, Catherine. *The Blue Cat of Castle Town.* (Countryman Paper, 1985)

Irving, Washington. *Rip Van Winkle.* (Little, 1988)

Levin, Betty. *The Keeping Room.* (Greenwillow, 1981)

Lindbergh, Anne. *The Hunky-Dory Diary.* (Harcourt, 1986)

Ormondroyd, Edward. *Time at the Top.* (Bantam, 1963)

Pascal, Francine. *Hangin' Out with Cici.* (Viking 1977)

Wood, Nancy. *Many Winters.* (Doubleday & Company, Inc., 1974)

Answer Key

Page 13
1. Accept appropriate descriptions.
2. Cottage was not inviting, visitors not welcome.
3. Wood appeared peaceful, as if it should not be disturbed.
4. They have looked the same for 87 years.
5. Little music box painted with roses and lilies of the valley.
6. Angry about always being told what and what not to do.
7. She had heard it many years before, and it was the music of elves.
8. Accept any appropriate answer.
9. Met Jesse Tuck.
10. Accept any appropriate answer.

Page 18
1. Kidnappers seemed friendly and had no intention of hurting her. Said they would return her home the next day.
2. Accept any appropriate answer.
3. It had come from Mae's music box.
4. They have not changed in 87 yrs. because they drank from a spring in the wood by Treegap.
5. See pages 38 and 39, Chapter 7.
6. They wanted her to understand the consequences.
7. Accept any appropriate response.
8. Jesse thinks of it as fun and good times. Miles more seriously, wary of consequences.
9. Tucks were messy, cluttered, dusty. Fosters were clean, neat, orderly.
10. They are afraid people would notice they never changed.

Page 21
1. metaphor
2. simile
3. simile
4. personification
5. simile
6. personification
7. simile
8. metaphor
9. personification
10. metaphor
11. metaphor
12. simile

Page 23
1. She was no longer afraid; loved the Tucks.
2. Gentle, kind, insightful, caring.
3. Life is ever changing.
4. The Tucks do not grow and change, they are not really living.
5. Everyone would come running for some spring water and everyone would stay the same forever. Life would go on without them.
6. They haven't had a chance to interact with other people in 20 yrs.
7. Drink from the spring when she turns 17 so they could go off together forever.
8. He didn't realize what had happened to him until it was too late.
9. Accept reasonable responses.
10. He would tell them where Winnie was in exchange for the ownership of the wood.

Page 26
1. 6.67, 6.15, 5.71, 5.33, 5.00
2. .44 hrs.
   .33 hrs.
3. a,b,c (answers will vary)

Page 28
1. Accept appropriate summaries.
2. His grandmother knew Miles's wife.
3. He recognized the tune of the music box.
4. Accept reasonable responses.
5. She felt she had to save the secret of the spring.
6. He longed to have a normal life span.
7. She would not be able to die and their secret would be revealed.
8. She did what she had to do because she loved the Tucks and felt it was right.
9. She was happy with herself, and other children respected her.
10. Accept reasonable and complete responses.

Page 33
1. Helped Mae escape in order to keep their secret.
2. Accept appropriate responses.
3. Both made decisions about who should have everlasting life. Winnie gave her gift because she cared, the man only wanted to have financial gain.
4. Accept reasonable responses.
5. He was glad she chose to live a natural life and remain part of the "wheel."
6. Answers may vary.

Answer Key *(cont.)*

Page 36

G	B	K	R	O	M	E	I	Q	D	L
1752	1770	1776	1787	1804	1861	1878	1884	1896	1901	1903

T	P	F	S	N	A	J	V	H	U	C
1914	1920	1939	1941	1952	1963	1964	1969	1977	1986	1990

Page 41

Intention: Winnie wants to make a difference in the world.

Initial Barrier: Winnie is stuck at home not able to do what she wants.

Barrier Reversal: Learns about Tuck and spring.

High Point: Loves Tucks.

Rug Pulling: Man with yellow suit wants the spring.

Catastrophy: Mae kills man.

Resolution: Winnie helps Mae escape.

Page 43

Matching: 1) Mae 2) Tuck 3) Jesse 4) Man in Yellow Suit 5) Winnie

True or False: 1) True 2) True 3) False. Although that is a matter of opinion, they knew the importance of keeping the spring a secret.
4) False. His idea would have cause irreparable damage to the world. 5) True.

Short Answer: 1) The music box. 2) Their cat did not drink and had a normal life. 3) He had followed the Tucks. 4) He saw her hit the stranger. 5) Summer storm.

Essay: Accept fully supported appropriate responses.

Pages 44 & 45

Answers will vary. Accept fully supported responses.

48